Rivering

Dean Kostos

SPUYTEN DUYVIL
New York City

Library of Congress Cataloging-in-Publication Data

Kostos, Dean.
Rivering / Dean Kostos.
p. cm.
Includes bibliographical references.
ISBN 978-1-933132-37-2
I. Title.
PS3561.O8432R58 2012
811'.54--dc23
2011046494

ACKNOWLEDGMENTS

Adirondack Review: "Standing Knife, Pinon, and Morning Glory"
American Literary Review: "Last Painting"
Bayou Magazine: "Tower of the Moment"
Assaracus: "Homage to Alan Turing"
Big City Lit: "How the Blue Intrudes"; "Saturnine," published as
    "Chamberlain of Tars"; "Person Walking through Enormous Dark
    House"; "Have the Dead Washed One Hand?"
Borderlands: Texas Poetry Review: "Phlegethon—River of Fire"
The Brownstone Poets Anthology: "Garden"
The Cimarron Review: "Nostalgia for Now"
The Cincinnati Review: "Myself to Myself: A Retrieved Photograph at
    Age Seven"; "Photograph of Myself, Age Four, Asleep in My
    Father's Arms"
Confrontation: "Her Lists"
The Dirty Goat: "Written in Hair"; "Miss Havisham"; the latter poem
    subsequently appeared in the anthology *Divining Divas*.
Ekphrasis: "Dwarf Pushing Pram"; this poem was subsequently
    nominated for a Pushcart Prize by the editors.
Euphony: "The Pharmacist's Shoes"
The Griffin: "Rivers of Hades"
HUBBUB: "Egyptian Cure for the Liver"

Inertia: "Bird in Unexplored Valley"; "Vision of a Maenad as
    She Goes Under the Sea"; "A Cow's Consciousness of Stars"
Minnetonka Review: "History Tilts across Your Hips," published
    as "The Kritios Boy."
Owen Wister Review: "Gradual Dissolve: Three Views of
    Eakins's Photographic Portrait of Walt Whitman"
Poetry in Performance: "Lesson"
Porcupine: "On the Difficulty of Reading Paul Celan"; "Hart
    Crane Before Drowning"
Reading Brokeback Mountain (anthology): "On Seeing
    Brokeback Mountain for the Sixth Time"
Red Rock Review: "Paper Ghost"; "One Among Many";
    "Reliquary Room"; "Even the Gods of Thought Have
    Thoughts: They Are Us"; and "Is Facelessness Modern?"
River Oak Review: "A Caterpillar"
The Same, "Liquifire"; "Ordnung"
Stand Magazine : "Adolescence"; "Wound"; "Can a Nighttime
    House Share a Daytime Sky?"
Stranger at Home (anthology): "Declensions"; "Radiant Liar";
    "Shores of Walker Lake"
Sulphur River Literary Review: "Words Unravel"
Talisman: "Gradations"
Vanitas: "Siena"
The Wallace Stevens Review: "Dusk over Hartford"
The Western Humanities Review: "Introducing John L. Sullivan";
    this poem subsequently appeared in *Pomegranate Seeds*.
Zone 3: "The Painter of Self-Portraits"

Rivering was a finalist for the Gival Press Poetry Award.

For Anna Kontogeorge

Contents

"It is possible that there is no other memory than the memory of wounds."
—CZESLAW MILOSZ

One

SHORES OF WALKER LAKE

an anonymous nineteenth-century photograph
of a Native-American boy

Come to water as to a page.
Point your fishing-rod and trawl,

scrawl the muddy floor. Reflection
swims into itself: bow meeting

bone—outline of a beak,
outline of another boy poking

his fishing-rod up
where yours impales

water's skin. Tilt your head
into his liquid shadow—

read his featureless face. One
becomes many:

ghost-shirts whorl like sage smoke.
Ghosts dissolve into a pollen trail,

past dogbane and amaranth.
Chants warble through the valley

where the dog-star web leads, where
you surely return.

The boy below the lake
waits, cawing the Nevada sun

to flood canyons with wraiths:
they feast on trout and bitterroot,

they feast on acorns and bergamot,
they feast on sweet cicely and violets,

their mouths erased like a smudge.

PHOTOGRAPH OF MYSELF, AGE FOUR, ASLEEP IN MY FATHER'S ARMS

A son is a valley, an undulation,
his arm a rivulet

curving round a sleeping doll.
In the world of dolls, he is an elder,

father of this glossy
homunculus.

There is a real father—hand
enfolding the boy.

The father is sleeping
too, face tilted down—illustration

in an ancient fable, chin pointed
into the open page of his white collar.

His eyelashes are eighth notes,
dark insects,

flying over the score of his face,
but such music is

unheard
in this diminished world

of worn surfaces. No buzz
of language—grammar of flies—

ever touches the father.
As he surrounds the boy

in the river of his arms,
it runs dry.

MYSELF TO MYSELF:
A RETRIEVED PHOTOGRAPH AT AGE SEVEN

You offer me a cloudy cat
barely contained in your arms:

left hand curled like a catalpa leaf
around furred shoulders, right hand

bracing the rump. Your pale sweater's collar
is a double V: stripes red and blue,

despite descending grays.
The Vs are victories that swallow your neck.

Your lips press together in a perpetual B,
stuttering the word "boy."

Your eyes blend
into mine the way twilight

swims with the diluted sun
as night prepares its questions.

Your eyes plead:
Is this enough? I offer you

what I've loved most—my friend
in his white cloak of fur. No,

no future caress will reveal
the adults behind: Mother

in wool suit and windowpane jacket;
Father in pleated slacks,

cinched by the brown belt
sometimes used on you, its buckle

a squinting eye. Who ripped the rest
of the photo away, the jagged halo

around you? When your eyes engage mine
in the commerce of cat,

I make the bones in my arms malleable,
bend them into the slender

black-and-white past—
accept your unanswerable gift.

A CATERPILLAR

*

is a thin zipper
adorned with gold-and-black beads
curving over leaves

color of nutmeg
and felt, color of a man's
suit as he hikes a

dusty road alone
on a film-noir summer dusk
film frames flickering

**

is a row of false
eyelashes dropped from one eye
inching, arching, its

glamour a grammar
unread and unseen as it
slinks from sight, beneath

a maple's fruit-wing
seed: dun paper disguises
a naked eyelid

***

is a swank comma
scrawled in Japanese with a
brush and ink, writhing

into a red rope
pulled from a magician's hat
now pulled taut into

the realm of language
now become an em dash but
not a period

WRITTEN IN HAIR

The Philadelphia Museum of Art

We clatter down marble corridors.
Squeezing my mother's hand, I climb
waves of stairs. The American Wing:
Shaker chairs hang from hooks—
skewered angels. Countenances
of grim men and women
enter our eyes like cold

knives. Samplers flank the wall—
colors of dried sweat and blood. Child
brides stitched crewelwork
with their hair: mottoes, ivy vines,
mustard seeds. I imagine a girl
spinning hair from her scalp, feeding
skeins into large-eyed

needles. When the sampler maker
unclasps the cloth, her wooden hoop
rolls along the corridors. Two years
older than I, that girl chases it,
apron untied and soiled, dark
hair loosened from bows. I run
to rescue the hoop from the precipice

of stairs. The girl's startled past speech, eyes
pleading, *Don't let it fall*, hand stitching air.
When I pass the hoop to her, she fits
her head into its maw. As if being unborn—
—or feeding herself to history—
she pulls in her legs, torso, arms,
till she and the hoop vanish.

LESSON

"Consider the word *drawing*," my art
teacher begins. "Think of it as drawing
something out as you draw lines on a newsprint
pad, leaving inessentials behind. Drawn

down the page, the form will seem to draw
itself, drawing the stem of a pear, rim of a bowl—
drawn because they have to be there, your stick
of charcoal drawing them like a kind of writing.

Draw what calls out to be translated
—the rumple of cloth, drawn with the side
of charcoal bits, saved in drawers. Let the arcs
of smudge draw out deeper lines, which define

and give depth to your drawing. Shadows become
a nest the still-life you've drawn can rest
into. Now draw in the mystery, press down harder—
let darkness draw all the elements together."

WOUND

He sees a shadow leak from his sleeve,
trickle dark as oil.

Grows certain
that if not attended to, it will accrue

till he is drenched in darkness.
Does not know its source.

Shakes his arm, but shadows,
like pain, dissolve when bidden,

so he invents a language
of hidden intentions—things he means

to say—obscured by a thicket
of divergent words, metallic on the tongue.

This is his ruse to coax the shadows into exposing
their origin, so he might stanch

their flow like hemophiliac
blood from a wound.

No avail. No kinship found
between the language of what happens

to happen and the clotted
grammar of what is devised.

ADOLESCENCE

a recurring dream

I am speaking to the tulips
      in shadows of suburban
décor. Tapering halls. Red
      bulbs slur the air,
submerge walls in liquid
      flame. Rows of shirtless
youths line the corridors. Torsos
      bloom as I pass.
I admire yet fear these men,
      desire and stalk them, our pupils
ravenous, blurred. Who's reaching
      inside me, uprooting tulips
grown without familiar light?
      I slog forward. The men's hands
rest on waists, fingers
      prying open flies.
Incandescence
      moistens the tulips. Parallel
along both walls, the youths ease
      down their jeans
in unison with my steps:

       down to dark deltas, down
to tender shoots.
       In diminishing light, the tulips
evaporate: the men
       dissolve into my sheets.

SATURNINE

I step onto Saturn's ring, revolve
among revelers. Black disks

spin. Boys and girls press into each other,
merge in chaperoned halls.

The music swells, skips.
I ... I ... I

fall from a noose, plunge into melancholy's
bubbling tars.

The door to the adolescent ward locks shut
with the finality of the boulder

rolled against Christ's tomb.
Winding sheets tighten.

I listen for the world's distant throbbing, watch
from safety-glass panes: faces

fracture, syringes hiss air into veins. Coke-bottle
shards carve a constellation

of scars.
Scents of ether and disinfectants.

After a shaman cauterizes patients' temples, he
sprinkles medicinal words

over my head, turns screws through my soles.
He commands me to dance, vexed

by my sullen stillness. But far from my padlocked
doors and stone wall, the dancers

still study New Math
and a ferocity that churns dust and ice

into nimbused rings.
Classroom windows slide open.

The students slant telescopes toward oblivion:
blood on the moon.

A stain, a stigma—
trace of who I had been.

DECLENSIONS

To learn a lexicon of remembering, I
            ransack clay jars, find sheaves

of things unwritten,
            unsaid. By the mouth

of a river, an angel alights,
            glints like ice.

He points to a syntax
            of fragments: handle-wing

of an urn, nimbus rim,
            plates with names of defunct

asylums, green-glass face
            that poured dark music:

coloratura submersion. Music,
            after all, is a form of drowning,

a half-forgotten grammar detaching itself
            from itself. As an ice sculpture

melts, his clear wings
            fill, fail, fall.

RELIQUARY ROOM

You're back—sitting at a bench in a stone dining-room,
among a dozen nuns.
Questions coil from mouths like plumes.

Now, the room's a laboratory: you've begun
to examine hand-blown
vials and amphorae, each one

infused with tiny bubbles, like roe. The crones
help you polish the bottles,
lofting them up to lamps—shown

to me? Jars hold body parts (given up without brutal-
ity) of infants and adults, even a muscled arm, bent
like the *Arm and Hammer* logo. The jars' mouths were portals

the hearts, eyes, and viscera went
through, poured like sangria. The only relics I can't see are
the thoughts. Igniting, they bend

into strips of smoke—memories charred:
some spiral, some break into Morse code,
depending upon the form of the jar

and the mind from which they curled. How odd—
these thoughts metamorphose,
having survived their brains. But here the dream erodes …

I know you're dead, as are, I suppose,
these nuns. Yet it might seem rude to ask
(the dead become defensive when roused

by such effrontery). You're holding a flask
containing your life and death: your face caving in,
the service, the funeral, the plot. I bask

in the past: you're alive again,
weighing relics that float
in luminous liquid. One ruined

urn in your care contains the rotting
remains of my lawyer father: his eyes
glare into me, noting

my desire to say the right word—not *say* … *imply*
my acquittal by a higher court. But
my mind goes blank—mute as *he* was before dying.

Other reliquaries, darkened to the color of walnut
stain, reveal portions of friends who kindled
the transformation from Now to Then. Eyes half shut,

you hold an ochre candle
to an amphora on an iron tripod. The glass
lid has a sphere for a handle.

As you lift the flame to the amphora and pass
your breath over its sides, I watch
ember-colored images—selves!—amass

against the glass from inside. At a touch,
their faces focus, shrivel
into others, then become blotches.

I no longer know them: dissolved!
Following some arcane sequence, Grandmother,
you place my empty jar on a shelf—question solved:

one self among rows of others.

HUGHES'S SUBJECTS

1. WOMAN OPENING A LETTER

Dangerous to be pared, to wear
no skin, no

       margin. Never thought I'd see
       his handwriting again. I've tended

a parched garden, avoided thorny
verdicts—roots knitting a tangled script.

       More than a generation,
       I have floated

       as dust into a wingchair,
       wingless. His envelope lies

among sheaves. Dangerous to be pared,
to wear no skin.

       As I slide the blade
       —curious Caesarian—

the envelope gives up its voice.
I could leave the letter unfolded,

unread. Instead, I unpleat
its indecisions. Mine.

Regret bleeds from cursive—
eyes flay the missive.

2. PERSON WALKING THROUGH ENORMOUS DARK HOUSE

I swim shadows, hair's dénouement
scrawling behind me.

>Shifting figures of dust—
>high, white sighs of it—dissemble,

disassemble.
When moon was milk, it flooded

>tall windows, guided my peregrinations.
>But I never arrived.

>Now, I dissolve, creak by
>creak, into crevices,

devices. Voices
bleed incriminations. I pad

>polished floors to quell the susurrus,
>the *no* of an abandoned child

who would not sleep
between covers

of a discarded book,
      her bones thinner than light.

3. MIDNIGHT IN A MOUNTAIN VILLAGE

Stars spike into ice, leak
          over steepled geometry.

Baize undulates more sensually
than a tear. While stars rinse

          houses, lungs heave: children
          sleep. Angry parents make love. Rivulets

          tattoo primordial rock.
          Their scrawl writes,

          unwrites histories
          unread.

          In a house lit by breath,
a man transcribes the clatter of icicles.

His pen scrapes the page's skin,
          abrades

its secrets. He writes the village
alive.

4. CHANGE OF VISION OF A MAENAD
AS SHE GOES UNDER THE SEA

Below,   we became families,
                                          become familiar.

                                          Colonies, culture.
In early years, I chanted backward

                                          into temples of burnished coral,
                                          alcoves shining.

Like a vibrating guitar string or sound waves
filling a flute, a returning force

pierced me: oscillations!
The sea sucked me into its magma.

But an equal force summoned
me to surface.

On soil, I patter with agnostic feet
and seem to belong

but know I never can.
The land dwellers can't emerald

my Sargasso, bubbles threading
dim arpeggios.

Although I chant with a flute's throat,
don't believe the sirens' myth.

Don't believe
a bloody froth hatched a goddess like a squid

or that she sprang
from her father's

castration. I knew no such mutilation,
no sanguine mousse   my awakening.

I was a handful of salt,
          passing through brink,

          my weight
          weightless. No fires burned.

I wanted light, breathing
          water.

5. COW'S CONSCIOUSNESS OF STARS

Milky stars dribble
over black sky-mountains.

        I count flecks while hands tug
        a dead calf from me,

then a live one. What difference?
I'll never lick it clean, never

           nudge it into tottering. My milk sluices
           into plastic tubes, sloshes

into vats. I exhale, blow out stars.
Abattoir.

Hands slaughter newborns: hooves ground
         into medicinal capsules, flesh

          pounded into pink pages,
          sautéed with butter, wine, capers.

What star has magic devious
         enough to reassemble those sheaves?

I'm not beguiled by stars.   Leave
                                                        that to humans. Let them

                lift their eyes to the sway
                of vaporous flames.

6. BIRD IN UNEXPLORED VALLEY

Explore, a form of conquer, comes before name.
    I'm nameless. Quills

    buoy me skyward, as they once buoyed
hands into writing: to name,

    to claim the thereby moment
    preceding *own*.

I soar above rapacious jaws.
A lizard unfurls its sticky tongue,

ensnares
ants, grasshoppers, slugs.

    Waters purl from volcanic stone, slide
from a Monstera leaf, trace

    nervure. A red-eyed toad squats,
unblinking. I've seen this from above,

    below. I perch at the methane
    maw of a cave,

at a sun-blind lake, at the cusp of no-
name. The cave sputters no syllable—

the only caw mine
as I explode into wing.

7. THE STONES OF THE CITY

Livid lacerations on gray.
Chisels etch our granite like hot blades
scarifying flesh.

Trains and cars grub
through our primordial hulk,
volcanic clay.

Sacrificed
into slab and tile, into entablature
and pillar, we

—the expendable stones—
vanish
into secular parabolas.

Dense as complicity,
we buttress skyscrapers.
Without our heft, our dark

schist, those stories would soon
relinquish their gleam.
Color of wind, color of mind.

NOSTALGIA FOR NOW

Sometimes I see people
and feel as if I've missed them
even though I may
never have met them before.

Say: the way a woman wears
a plum-colored scarf over an old leather jacket
inspires *It's so good to see her again,*
but I have never seen her before.

Or: when I spot a young, unshaven
man for the first time—trundling
an encased cello down the street
on its wobbling wheel—

it's as though I were peering
through memory with great nostalgia:
this moment in September, this wind,
this peculiar green tinge of light.

Two

THE PAINTER OF SELF-PORTRAITS

All flesh is neutral, she said,
no matter how dark, how

frail. Just look at Chardin,
that great painter of browns.

Neutrals resist the stir
of palette knife. Complexioned

anticipation. Kindled
blush. Summoned to surface,

warmth meets her hands
as she presses toward a landscape:

slope of tawny shale, fish-
spine pattern of pines—

a landscape glazed on canvas,
glossed with linseed oil.

One has traveled far,
she said, swimming into a mirror.

IS FACELESSNESS MODERN?

after Monet's

Woman with Parasol Turned Toward the Left

The painter asked,
so I planted myself here, waiting

en fin de siècle. Blue-and-white bandages
scumble through sky. My toile skirt

billows toward a future.
My breath blooms

color of hydrangeas.
Scrawling roots

suture me to soil. Grass teems
with questions, warnings

I won't bend to read.
Can almost see the next century—

shimmering hallucination.
Can't look away.

Though the past nudges
my back, I block it

with the lime-green rind
of my parasol, step

over the border into
the present. Now,

I'm the future's sacrifice, my face
an immaculate wound.

HISTORY TILTS ACROSS YOUR HIPS

> In The Kritios Boy, *the human form takes a revolutionary step*
> *out of the block of marble, turning his head and escaping the*
> *restraints of centuries.* —Nicholas Gage

Blank-eyed boy, what have you seen,
        you who speak through your eyes'

hollows—each one a mouth, exhaling
        daimons of wind?

You've learned the art of tying
        air into knots. Learned to see

distances lit by wounds.
        Ravines perilous as love.

Metallic embroideries glint
        in diminished lamplight.

When your eyes speak, one talks
        of arrivals, the other

of departures, each a tunnel
        away, your thoughts unspooling

toward the vanishing point.
                Falling to the ground, your chiton

reveals the first *contrapposto*, before the word.
                Want surges into laurel-spine, branching

into shoulders, neck, face. Beneath your snowy
                chest, heart-roots snap

from muscles' memory: harp-strings
                plucked. A lover cups the warmth

of your manhood. One eye: *Leave*;
                the other: *Stay, stay.*

STATUE IN THE LINE OF PERSPECTIVE

As if freeze-framed by the lens
    of Muybridge,

ice-glossed statues creak: interrupted
    procession.

When I pass a stone figure,
    his halted cadence

subsumes my own.
    Bent leg. Blued vein.

Evening locks me into itself—
    dim air sculpts

space between branches.
    Sky a clay-gray density.

Above that granite vein,
    sweat trickles to ankle,

pedestal, swag,
    gashed pomegranate.

A *daimon* surges up from soil,
      up through my guts

like a circular saw. I am split,
      un-numbed.

This glazed tableau glisters
      in wind. Another trickle …

In a minute, or thirty-five
      years, a flesh foot sheds

its hull, a shin its casements:
      thigh   heart   mouth.

GRADUAL DISSOLVE: THREE VIEWS OF EAKINS'S
PHOTOGRAPHIC PORTRAIT OF WHITMAN

1891, a year before Whitman's death

I.

Does he still see carrion flies
glitter over dead mouths?
Does he still hear wives weep,
weep no more, dirges

smudging air? Outbreak
of liquefaction. Sweat glazes his brow.
The upright posts of his chair
and the window to the left incandesce,

vermeered.
Delft tiles in the background blur
with the pollen of moths
as the poet grasps the chair's carved

arms, his clothes and cloak
a layered dalmatic.
Anchorite or pagan?
I imagine scents

of ruffed mushrooms, lilacs, chrism.
Now, the background is molten:
window-light bathes
the left side of his pate,

ragged hair, splintered
        beard—
radiance taking him
        apart.

II.

He glows bronze
as the arms of gaunt soldiers,

while the posts of his chair
lose outlines, the window to the left,

a reflection of fire on tin.
The room behind him gutters

straw-colored and other psyches,
morning-scattered. Pressing the fluted wood,

his fingertips blanch, his knuckles
linden-bark.

His cloak is a cultivation
of gray flames, a cauldron of wounded

voices seeping round his ears.
Mystic or Corybant? I imagine scents

of beeswax and boiled milk.
When pane-light anoints his pate,

he dissolves, dipped in the moment
after death—smudged hair, corroded beard,

waves   thrashing.

III.

Plunged in the vessel, a lachrymatory—

bone-colored hair, eyes mute—he grows

waxen: flesh of dying

soldiers. The chair assumes a skeletal sheen.

The frail window a portal

of all past tenses: conversations were.

They whir,

haloed with carrion flies, embered eyes.

He wears a frayed cassock—cloth

soft as an eyelid.

Votary? Voluptuary?

Scents: ashes,

whiskey, yew needles.

When pane-light anoints

his temples, he dissolves

in a font—moon mane, sun beard

—radiance plashing:

Drink deeply, drink.

HART CRANE BEFORE DROWNING

This is my mother—as far as the eye can see.
I have ridden her turbulences
and become them.

This is the summer air that tasted my voice,
feeding it back to me,
scalded, salted, bleached.

This is day's star: cynosure
I have followed to arrive
unraveled. No,

the sun is not a ball of barbed wire,
but a bleeding tangle of nerves. I have written
it that way in this deceitful

radiance, this hunger bending back on itself to eat
itself, till I am all that remains. Staring
into lapping waters, I see a reflection: a young sailor's

clothes draped over my chair like a futtock shroud;
I feel his stubble, chest hair, nipples,
the satin of his foreskin.

But memory immolates itself, hurled
like an Aztec sacrifice—
down steps leading toward dissolution.

As sun slants its whisky-hue—waves intoxicating—
I hear the thrashing swell of arrivals:
once-again-never-again . . .

There will be no more taste
of sperm and blood, no more trysts disavowing
me with fists at dawn's spill.

I have fulfilled this contract
with a bottomless force
and drink my mother in.

INTRODUCING JOHN L. SULLIVAN

a painting by George Bellows

What no one seems to notice is the way
the tuxedoed announcer's jaw is a cup
from which he pours confidence into himself.
His grayed whiteness tapers into the sheen
of his lapel as another man noses
his face into his ear. This second man
tilts his own thigh slightly, with the lilting
kick of a showgirl, as if in offering.

What no one might want to notice is the referee's
gesture—something like a sneeze, the last
gasp of someone shot in the back,
or the raised hand of a *heldentenor*
shifting from recitative to aria. Even his mouth
is open—not to speak, but to sing
in words whose every vowel is "ah."
What the referee, in the tentativeness of his gesture,

pretends not to notice is the promoter,
who looks as though his head could lift off
from his shoulders like the lid from a teapot—
a ceramic man, the fold in his suit, his collar

and lapel are glazed onto him. The hat
he's holding is an open mouth
to swallow the song, if indeed it is a song,
or only the yawp of the man beside him.

What everyone must notice is the seated boxer
—his swelling calves and sweating biceps—Mr. Sullivan
sitting in the champ's corner of the ring.
Tousled bangs shade deep-set eyes. Or are they
black and blue? He thanks a man (bent in half
like a maître d') who's handing him something.
The two hands merge in one
continuous form like a scroll of paper unrolling.

What everyone might want to ignore
is the bald man: Sullivan's trainer.
His hand curves over the boxer's pale
shoulder, his shaded face breathing words
into Sullivan's ear. Does the trainer want
to caress the boxer? Whatever he
wants, he finds intimacy in being useful
and accepts this role.

What no one notices is the nothingness hung
above the ring like an iron fist, the color
of annealed metal cooling, now cold.
This quadrant of darkness rises
above the referee, above the promoter,
above the trainer, even above Sullivan himself,
casting a stain over the clutter of crowd below,
over you and me, seated there in the second row.

LAST PAINTING

after Arshile Gorky

Pictogram of a dislocated soul,
                    this painting awaits

translation.   Brush strokes swash.
Foreground lunges,   background

                    crumbling into ash:
death marches, horseshoes hammered

onto feet.   Flayed legs
                    of children.

The painter dry-brushed the canvas
black and gray, scouring

memory. But the past seeped in: yellow
                    shone through the kitchen window

                    where he consoled his mother.
Green sprouted from charred soil,

below a moldy sun.
Red scribbled: fires, blood,

shriveled kisses.   He tried to say goodbye, but paint
                                   eluded him, coagulated

onto mirrored shards, knifed
in a circle, reflecting an empty room,

                           where he swung—
                           tongue of a mute bell.

ON THE DIFFICULTY OF READING PAUL CELAN

Plague of eyes.
Blood the color of fermented
blackberries. A mother's blood

is a more specific color, closer
to chamber music, violin-sweat,
old-fashioned perfume, even a voice

in a distant room. Her wounds
are not an end, not a bleeding past
the vanishing-point, past the line-

break. A mother's faded blood
marshals intuition, lures a poet of eyes,
of witnessing, of mourning, to crack

open German with a grackle-
beak. Magnolia-claws. He uses the tongue
of the Powerful to forge an unfinished

architecture of words—its domes
and buttresses—to will them into form,
a shelter that does not. The inner sentence,

I've come to see, is always unfinished.
Knowing this truth, a boy
stands outside an abandoned house,

looking up at its broken windows, his hands
clasped, his voice calling to reclaim
someone whose absence infects, infects …

DUSK OVER HARTFORD

Through shattered windows, the sea surface
    paraphrases the moon. *Farewell*
        to Florida—the men here are falling,

reads a postcard in an abandoned store.
    The men had no way of knowing
        ghosts would someday address

the United Dames: "Adieu, adieu!"
    Beneath a hotel ceiling fan, a widow stirs
        a tall drink; the American sublime

plays sad strains of a waltz. After all,
    life is anecdote, windows dimming
        with dense violet light. In its tint,

her mind proclaims fear the emperor,
    its shadow flapping large above her,
        as she sips tea in the lobby. A bird

with coppery, keen claws, it inscribes
    poetry's destructive force onto the mahogany
        table where the woman rests

her cup, its mark a nimbus.
    The narcotic sun lights
        six significant landscapes

outside the window.
    Outside the widow's
        mind, a man approaches.

She rasps, "Peer through my monocle and you'll agree
    a good man has no shape, but is various
        versions of the same poem."

EKPHRASTIC POEMS BASED ON IMAGINARY ARTWORK

I. PAPER GHOST

after Harunobu's woodblock print
Man Dressed as a Ghost

They pierce our souls with night-colored thread ...

We hear what we see: winds swoon
round our ankles like winding sheets, pulled

by ginger-root hands
of the dead. Chrysanthemum stalks

snag embroidered colors: *kiiro, kuro, midori.*
Scribbled with prayers, wooden plates rattle

from a roadside pagoda. A man murmurs
to himself. What is he saying?

"They pierce our souls with night-colored thread."

The man hears rain approach and runs
beneath the eaves of a Shinto shrine.

He'll wait there until the rain stops babbling;
he'll wait until the black ink ceases to bleed.

A crinkle marks his feeble steps, for
upon his white-paper hat, vest, pants

he's painted dendritic characters
to warn the living: *In the rustle*

of leaves, ancestors speak.
Flocking in trees, they pierce

our souls with night-colored thread.

II. DWARF PUSHING PRAM

after Manet's In the Park

Like a palette knife, light slices through sycamores,
greening her face.

Is she embarrassed the painter exposed
her choice:

a world of diminution—caretaker
of infants and children?

Among them
she stands tall. Invited past

her fragile smile, my eye glides over flesh
sheer as a rancid pepper.

Her forehead creases with the suspicion:
lack of stature is a flaw.

Although she'll never speak
such things, a patois of brushstrokes

implies the baby is not hers.
We cannot see its face.

Is the dark *voiture d'enfant*
empty?

Manet—master of black, off-black,
gray—situated this little woman

among cradling folds of indigo wool.
Her hem whispers along the flagstone:

Shecomesshegoesshecomesshegoes.
Look beyond her: people peek

below hats, behind fans,
above newspapers' serrated edges.

Because they know what she knows,
but will not offer the bravery

of stares, she remains captive
of her suspicions. Forsaken,

, she retreats into being needed: rocking
the carriage, cooing a lullaby.

She imagines her song can summon
the sun to dissolve into darkness

like butter in an iron skillet.
Soon it will spill

onto someone else's morning.
Soon the child will grow too tall.

III. THE PHARMACIST'S SHOES

after de Chirico's Allegory of the Shoes

A skin of dust covers this pair of stained
shoes, inside a tall armoire.

Shoetrees, cashmere coat, hat,
eyeglasses: possessions of the bald

pharmacist. Lined up like words
in a sentence—subject, verb, direct object

—his items describe the pharmacist
in sotto voce. His wife makes sure

his things have not been moved—even the dust
is intact. She places a doll version

of him among his effects and arranges framed
photographs on the shelf with his shoes.

She slides the herringbone jacket,
the one he used to wear to their favorite French

restaurant, revealing a door
in the back of the armoire. She opens it and sees

a torch-lit piazza. How often they strolled
there after the opera and a good meal. Tonight

she walks alone. The eyeless,
reclining statue ogles her, no, *them.*

She's with her husband
again. They've finished eating veal sautéed with capers,

and he just spilled red wine on his cordovan
shoes. Hand-in-hand, the pharmacist

and his wife pass a pharmacy. In its window
a ghastly reflection appears: an angry man

approaches the bald pharmacist, thrusts
a dagger into his chest, punctures his heart.

Like warm rose petals, blood splatters
onto his shoes. As the man and woman watch

in horror, her husband disappears
again. She crosses the piazza

—the eyeless statue still staring—then shoves
clothes aside on the rod, stepping

out of the armoire, careful
not to disturb the stained shoes.

IV. ONE AMONG MANY

after Romare Bearden's Young Man Caught in a Continuum

Faces and faces, no ...
masks collage a cacophony
of selves. Yet this collective "I"
faces and faces no-

where, because it turns in
every direction, in every era:
Nubia to West Africa, Mississippi to Harlem.
Because they turn into

voices, they bleed songs, spirituals, dirges.
Notice how one youth seems to approach,
the shadow-pattern of leaves flickering across dark skin.
Voices bleed songs, spirituals. Dirges

are heard even in times of rejoicing.
The boy continues to approach, never arriving
as his image multiplies into mouths.
Are they heard even in times of rejoicing?

V. HER LISTS

after Balthus's In a Room She Seldom Leaves

Her body's a box: elbows glued to floor,
knees dug into carpet, shoulders
level with hips, palms pressed
against papers to keep secrets

from seeping away. She wonders,
Can I trust my mind? Did I lock the door,
unplug the iron, blow out the candle
guttering under the portrait of a saint?

Check: yes; check: yes; check: yes.
Did I? Look again. She lines up geometries
of lists: table, chair, wall,
the patterns on her blouse, designed

to hold her thoughts in place.
Filed away. But again raptors
—venom shimmering from beaks—flock
between shadows, shrieking:

Robbers will ravage,
the iron will unfurl flames, devouring
the walls, the building, the block.
Your fault, all your fault.

The beiged order collapses, her mind
crimson: *flee!* When she can no
longer bear her defeated self, shame
descends. Veil of tatted insect legs

she can't pry from her face. Soon she
will scoop up scraps of thought, tuck
them back into lists,
the lined papers—bars, bars …

MISS HAVISHAM

Lace. I will hoard it, color
of tarnished mirrors and mold.
Lace tatted by eyelash-
legs of spiders. And now
lace conceals everything—
windows, rancid wedding cake,
my eyes.

But instead of webs
weaving a curtain—a scrim
obscuring sight—they filter all
I see: I now know what will
never cross the wizened
threshold of self.
No one

will suckle my arid breasts,
no man, no infant.
Below the window, urchins
spit my name, "Hag!"
From the ivory satin flounces
of my gown, from the sugared tiers,
I scrape

rat droppings with my nails.
The cake-top figurines
have long since collapsed
into rotten avalanches,
wedges of icing—mortar
sealing a house, a room,
a life.

ORDNUNG

in Amish tradition, a set of unwritten laws

A sole
black surrey—dark
as the brim of the man's
hat—canters down a dusty road.
Sudden

twist. The
austere surrey
disappears. To the left:
a wheat field; to the right: corn. Crows
scatter

into
stratus: hundreds
of black gloves peel away
the cloud quilt. Beneath it—annealed
pewter.

ON SEEING *BROKEBACK MOUNTAIN*
FOR THE SIXTH TIME

When Jack watches Ennis vanish
through his rearview mirror, that sphere

of disappearance becomes a tunnel, drawing
me back into the film.

Again the projector's beam
magnetizes dust into hands and mouths:

tongues taste tongues,
tasting the fractured crumbs

of words not spoken,
inhaled. Every cusp of red

nuance impels me like a fist pushing
living tissue through a sieve.

Perhaps the best that desire can offer
is to carve a phantom silhouette of the beloved—

outline of a murdered body.
But this crimson has no

consequence—flesh, act, and lie
translated to ash.

Jack's bloody shirt no longer smells
of cigarettes, sweat, sweet hay;

even the ghost of scent has abandoned
Ennis. As winds roil dust

past matchstick houses, searching
for codes lost

in the folds of remembering,
shirts embrace.

HOMAGE TO ALAN TURING

Because God would be a Mathematician, computing trees
to branch, leaves to uncurl,
ferns to unfurl—

Because you saw a pine-cone configure its pangolin-petals
into the meter of Sanskrit
prosody—

Because the Fibonacci Series spiraled, arcs connecting
corners, swooping into characters,
a language—

Because arcane ciphers buzzed in a Nazi contraption
(*Satan ex machina*) you pressed your brain
to that malevolent whir—

Because you bent over Enigma at the Government
Code & Cipher School,
defending England—

Because Gödel's Incompleteness Theorem
named an uncaused cause beyond containment,
you magicked an oracle in a box—

Because you endowed the electronic mind
with spinning cryptograms, a vernacular
of brainwork—

Because you created "Colossus" to decipher codes,
win a chess game, expound a theology
of hissing stars—

Because you watched *Snow White & the Seven Dwarfs*,
a prince emerged, silvered
in an all-seeing mirror—

Because you were sex as well as cortex, your eyes
fell on a young man who materialized
out of Manchester's fog—

Because his tousled hair and immaculate flesh
solidified out of rain and desire,
an elemental sacrament—

Because you loved a man, you were deemed criminal.
Even as Europe pardoned Nazis, you faced sentencing:
prison or chemical castration—

Because you chose the latter, your manhood and its desires
retracted. You grew breasts
beneath your tweed vest—

Because you sank into darkness, tumbling from England
and the world, your voice crumbled
into inaudible ciphers—

Because you injected Eve's fruit with cyanide
and bit into its skin, you were ensorcelled
in a swoon, dissolving

into a blank screen, a matrix of transistors,
phosphor throbbing with the world's
intelligence—

Because the Apple logo now bleeds with your poisoned
saliva, your mouth crusted with decades
of silence—

Because I can love another man, and because this world
all too willingly forgets, I thank you, writing this
on a computer.

HAVE THE DEAD WASHED ONE HAND?

Sparrows rinse their wings in pools of dust.
Do the dead begin like good children,
meaning to wash their hands?
Is it slower for some, the ones
who chafe on satin shirrs?
Do the dead—in their battle with soil—
lave from flesh and memory
all that once clung, all that said *I have*?
Some dead wash invisible wings
in muddy thaws of March
before their flesh flakes—
gold leaf from an icon.
Some dead bathe only one hand
before entering the cathedral of bones.

Three

TOWER OF THE MOMENT

beginning with a line by Kenneth Rexroth

A dark blur in the blur of brightness
spreads faster than hands bend neon
into language, faster

than questions reconstruct themselves
into the tower of the moment.
Memento of the day

before tomorrow, where we watch moisture
thread its music into prophecies
once discerned in the guts of animals

sacrificed. You recount fables
read as a child, remembered as Braille
on the cortex, texture

of wormholes. Moon-plucked waves
leap toward the bluffs above memory,
site of your childhood home—sight

of agon, ago. The crushed model
of a lighthouse, its light extinct.
So much for reconstructing ruins.

You sit there among them, trying
to decipher a leaf's nervure,
the trees' inflamed nerves illuminating

night sky. So many wires,
names, voices … America
was falling through a whisper.

CAN A NIGHTTIME HOUSE SHARE A DAYTIME SKY?

Can you plant sambas in my bed?
　　Have they the texture of trickling stones?

Do shirts converse with the bodies that wore them?
　　Is a CD disk a reliquary of gray voices?

How many arms do I need to dance with an octopus?
　　Is the helix inside the sun its spine?

Can you measure the downbeat of a leaf stung with rain?
　　Is a tolled bell a terrified eye?

Why destroy the silver fire of spider webs?
　　In what direction do a table's claw-legs point?

GARDEN

For Daniel Simko

Painted with wet ash, your portrait
     is bright

with expectation—light cast by flowers'
     stigmata.

Throats of lilies caw: *Now ...*
     no. Each word becomes a Hebrew *yod,*

a Tarot tear falling: both rain
     and ray. There are realms

where these are equal. In your adopted
     country, an eagle curves talons

round an unfinished pyramid,
     an omniscient eye

weeping. And you and I, though we
     never knew each other,

return to our respective exiles,
     to dig in arid soil,

to plant ashes, coaxing
suns to bloom.

WORDS UNRAVEL

What fires burn green,
          emerging from the lint of winter?

What shadows sprout vines,
          unfisting waxen leaves?

What flames filigree—a convolvulus
          twisting round wrought-iron bars?

What snowy words unravel
          from white kimonos, only then to melt?

RADIANT LIAR

*In ancient Rome, the moon was spoken of
as a liar,* luna mendax, *because its form
resembled a C when waning* (decrescere) *and
a D when waxing* (crescere).

My face a moon in phase,
my first quarter an Art Deco
eyelid. Profile to the left—
a George Hurrell photograph.

Despite my box-office
draw, I chug phosphorescence
to quell the chronic dark.
When Shadow Side taunts:

"Liar," I lunge at her throat
with an opal blade. Her shrieks
ricochet like twanged metal. I
try to ignore them, strum

my lyre's platinum strings,
fingertips bleeding.
In a silver-ingot
chamber, I bathe in Harlow light,

sprawl across gray
satin sheets. Night-
blooming herbs intoxicate
brain's crenellations. Cure

my insomnia—this febrile
film noir, this waning
into C *(cannot)*, this swelling
into D *(do not)*.

NIGHT'S GLASS BOWL

Nut, many-breasted goddess, arches over the parched
world, her torso tattooed with stars, her nervous system
stretching across the cosmos—   *trundle them*

constellation of nipples. Stars
awl the dark. She breathes
through the illuminated stabs.   *to a practicum*

A celestial X-ray exposes ghost-
bones of her sons and scions:
When Osiris wears his father's   *brushes*

crown of asps, Seth hacks
and dismembers his brother. *Nut*
harvests the green corpse, scattered   *whisper away*

throughout the province, her droplets streaking
night's glass bowl. She mixes a paste
of loam, herbs, tears. Smears   *silt*

the unguent, sutures all that's torn.
Dominion of rags (heal them).
Pinions of falcons (wield them).   *dust*

Keening her mother's ancient spell, *Nut* breathes
fumes over Osiris'
disheveled brains. His crown   *words*

slithers among hops and grains, silt
and salt glistening on his eyelids.
The Nile's mouth is *Nut*'s grin.   *clay*

RIVERS OF HADES

I. Acheron—River of Woe

Enthralled by body's
        avarice, unbeings drub
my muddy banks: dip
        toes, press lips, lick my wrinkling
        skin. Vapors blur the swash:

so much ectoplasm …
        Not forms—silhouettes
of voices retreating
        from speech, drained into a pool
        of refusal. Faces spurn

reflections: a mouth
        spheres *No*; a man breaks a glass;
a syringe shimmers
        into blunted flesh. Cannot
        peer into their own eyes: hold

up withered hands to
        be shielded. Though I send red-
footed falcons to
        hover, though I invoke wild
        poppies and birthroot to sprout,

astonishing them
     with color, they stare away,
slump past: neither dead
     nor breathing, neither meat nor
     shade, guzzling tears. Scuttling off.

II. Phlegethon—River of Fire

Who decreed fire and water opposites?
And did he walk the turquoise-tiled

paths, labyrinths leading to the Mysteries,
to the wall of oily flames

inhabited by being? Addressed
me in a fiery glossolalia,

demanded immersion—myself
within myself to be renewed, dissolved

in the blaze of my own knowledge. I saw
fire-flowers lose

their transparency, melt
into a blood-boil, ancient

as the world's body, liquefying
in red magma. I heard the naked

hum of the laburnum.
Where do my currents lead?

What is my destination?
Ranks of hissing waves:

fangs scald and gnash—
I the offering, I the flame.

III. Lethe—River of Forgetfulness

Saw, was …
I was what my eyes drank,
reflected palaces and gardens—

illusions all. I swirled through chutes
in my pupils, became a darker
music, vibrations submerging

thought. Heard there
undersong, undercurrent
and recoiled. What remained

dissolved, liquefaction of words:
chronicles spattered
with drunken nibs,

spoken, psalmed, keened.
Voices swayed over me—
braided currents. Was, saw:

Caw of blue jays.
Fleshy hydrangeas.
Silk of a lover's wrist.

Sealed the voices
in a sweating ewer of clay,
quaffed what was,

seen, desired until mouths
—colossal zeroes—
gnawed at margins

of the earth. *Unsee, undo,*
exhortations, until I too
was unseen, undone.

IV. Cocytus—River of Lamentation

Such music a drowning,
voices whorled before dissolution,
sluiced by sobs.
My waters bear the imprint:
squalls incised like grooves
on shellac. And like a disc

I circle darkly, repeat
howls of slain villagers and soldiers
who beheaded them; cries
of children plague-disfigured;
shriek of a man saber-cleaved.

A seamstress, missing her long-dead
husband, chants to Charon, *Chare mou,*
pare me. He
draws her closer with web-like

filaments. All lamentation
mine, my voice that texture—
embroidered dissonances:

black vines and buds
on white absence.

Each voice a taste.

V. Styx—River of Oaths

Nine is the number that cancels itself.
    I've traveled Hades nine times
        never, till time dissolved

itself. Those who break oaths
    breathed over my waves
        suffer nine years of thunder,

lightning, earthquakes. Listen to Charon's oars
    plashing: busy tonight.
        As he glides across my onyx,

his eyes flash
    ciphers. Drunk on rancid swill,
        his passengers squat

in cages of bone. Fools!
    Ignorant of the penalty for defiling
        my shores, they snivel,

"We will—we promise."
    Why should Charon believe them?
    Why should I?

Tonight, as they sail my black tides,
    I send harpies
        to chew their flesh—knitted

to memory like muscle to bone.
    Soon, the passengers will be flayed
        to fumes. Soon,

they'll reach their destination.
    When Charon roils my ooze,
        a whirlpool will spell

their names, my gulfs swallowing them
    down—nine times nowhere. Now
    here.

LIQUIFIRE

How often a thing recalls its opposite:
a sky with cloud-frills resembles sea.
The roiling blue, the froth-white swells
ebb into distant, aquamarine night.
Or consider how dawn and twilight
mirror each other. Both entrances tell
us the mauve passage is transitory.
As a boy I watched a bloom of blue, lit
on the stove, the watery flames a *liquifire*.
Even tears, when heard third-person,
can sound like paroxysms of laughter.
But if they're yours, they focus neither after
nor before, but *during*, in the frisson
of grief or joy. It's labels we acquire.

GRADATIONS

1.

Once, the only occurrence of
what-was was what
bread became after
immersion in wine.

2.

Before the race was won,
speed was the one thing
to remain hidden
from historians' pens.

3.

To be
unrelated to the arrow's speed
and to earth's axis is
to be.

4.

Schadenfreude
in ancient Egypt was
the quality of shade cast
by the Sphinx's nose.

5.
Her nose, shot off by one
of Napoleon's myrmidons,
still casts a shadow,
bringing joy to some.

6.
The quality of barking
versus the singer's craft
exists in a moment
music disavows.

7.
Height reached its apex,
curving back in time:
figure-eights incised in ice
made decisions accordingly.

8.
Fire, it once was written,
doused itself at the hour
when a neighbor no one
could see wept sweet tears.

9.
Descending from the mountain's lip,
the Pythia wore nothing
but the mousseline smudge
of synonyms for *yes*.

10.
Her movement was the fate
called Everything—
the shadow of each footstep
pleating innumerable stairs.

EVEN THE GODS OF THOUGHT HAVE THOUGHTS: THEY ARE US

I-Accept

is a town where winds scour abandoned maternity wards. Wearing the sound of children's voices, like *commedia dell'arte* masks, deranged mothers wait for a weathervane to point toward deliverance. Iridescent granules of rust scatter as a copper eagle spins.

How-Could-They?

lives in a small house like the one a cuckoo revisits in its forced trajectory, feet bolted to the revolving path on the clock's façade. The only décor is a mirror. As the cuckoo's mouth opens to repeat the eponymous marking of time, the splayed beak eclipses its face—the mirror unseen. But the clock has no dominion, for a place without deviations is a place without time.

I-Don't-Know

is a palace with porous walls and floor-to-ceiling windows. Scenery outside has been filmed and continuously rotates on screens. Voices, bird chirps, even so-called boating accidents, are prerecorded. Although the inhabitants breathe what they believe to be ocean air, looking onto the seaside community below—it's artificial. The dwellers know only what they are meant to know. Could the growth they feel as a green tingling in their nerves be real, nonetheless?

EGYPTIAN CURE FOR THE LIVER

The nerve which controls the pen winds itself
about every fibre of our being, threads the heart, pierces the liver.
—Virginia Woolf

Take one baby pigeon, armored beak
    weighing down its head—
        bantam bald man.

The bird quivers,
    flesh translucent
        through fern-like feathers.

Disheveled hut:
    inchoate body a sketch
        begun, or a drawing erased,

replaced by a smudged halo.
    What is the hum of blur?
        What is its weight?

Hold squab to liver;
    feel the exchange of matter.
        Paroxysm of molecules.

The prescriptive bird drinks
        in disease with every breath,
                every cell; soaks up virulence.

The purifying organ, restored
        to magenta, becomes
                a satin chamber

into which a presence pads:
        hush, hush ...
                The pigeon dies of the patient.

COLOR CHANT

after a Navajo chant for healing

Deity of sound and color—enter
house of silver under-leaf,

house of delirious firefly, house of fallen
claws. Collect them to unhook

stars. Your footfall drums, a flute breathing
above you. Deity

of undersong and ember, for you I clutch
a book of birch bark.

For you my voice blooms
vermilion. Restore my liver

to live. Restore *yes* to my eyes.
Deity of dirge

and pigment—with a carved box
of dreams, I walk.

Toward chanting waters, I walk. Bandaged
in ocher leaves, I walk.

From broken bells, I flee. From bones ground
into bread, I flee.

From the red deluge, I run. May I run past shadows'
boundary. Deity of cries

and marigold petals, I rise between two rivers.
May it be mountain-blue before me,

slate-blue behind me, rain-blue above me. May it be
sea and wind all around me.

In the stinging of color it began—in the ripening
of chant it has finished.

HOW THE BLUE INTRUDES

Tat tvam Asi (*Thou art That*)

—*The Upanishads*

Loosen self from self in the sweep
of green unknowing,
           in leaf-web,

branch, bark, loam. Once
there were names: river birch,
           bur, hornbeam.

But today my eye strays
from language, past
           branches' Linear B,

past their etched crosshatching,
their Baroque cartouche,
           the bronze disk sinking

into dark.
Sky ignites sapphire.
           Give in

to its ferocity of blue,
its bewildering
           That.

STANDING KNIFE, PINON and MORNING GLORY

a sculpture by James Surls,
Charles Cowles Gallery, New York

Knife, be my source. Cleave.
          Be root, a surge. Wooden knife,
              rise, rise into pine.

But your tree has wings
          embracing absence—become
              undone, the wire bloom

an aural-outline.
          A phonograph's horn, it pipes
              music from magma:

green the sound, mute the
          color drenching what eye hears,
              what ear recalls. Can't

a morning glory
          coax and curl with sweet hissing?
              Knife, be my source. Cleave

to, from. Be perfect
          kundalini. Energy
              arcs: a cobra's hood.

The spine of spirit
　　　is the portrait remaining
　　　　　when a blade flays form.

SIENA

Go to Siena. But only if it's stitched without boundaries,
if cypresses taper into finials, if

tamarisk and olive trees silver their vowels,
if racing banners ignite their flaming petals,

if you know which terminal will take you.
Go to Siena where a zebra-

striped Duomo will meet you, where a campanile
will toll: *SO-full, SO-full.*

There used to be so much of Siena, no one could hear
each breath crucified by the moon.

Where are the beloved faces?
What lightning bolt devoured them?

Black Death seared flesh, mouths
speaking blood.

Now, questions echo through vaulted halls.
A nun anoints weeds,

tendrils knitting into passageways,
into aquifers,

into the late-night café *L'Orfeo*. Boys on Vespas
reconfigure themselves in red

then reappear in cloaks of snow,
in crocus hoods.

When a gardener beheads antiphonal
sunflowers, Siena bleeds

from a carafe, overflows a fountain, coils
into illuminations.

There's so much of Siena, the threads
that once embroidered its banners

have tangled. A seamstress with wounded
fingers cuts it along the seams.

Gardeners, tailors, priests scissor bodies
from souls, hacking perforations—

Siena gurgling each name from the mouth
of its underground river.

NOTES

Rivering is adapted from this line in James
Joyce's *Finnegans Wake:* "Beside the rivering waters of,
hitherandthithering waters of. Night!"

"Hughes's Subjects": the titles in this series were
prompts Ted Hughes had created for Sylvia Plath, but for which
she never wrote a poem. "As was their custom, whenever Plath
experienced writer's block, Hughes wrote out lists of poem
subjects, often accompanied by astrological doodles," *No Other
Appetite: Sylvia Plath, Ted Hughes, and the Blood Jet of Poetry*,
edited and compiled Stephen C. Enniss and Karen V. Kukil.

"The Stones of the City" was taken from Hughes's
prompt: "The Stones of the City—Their Patient Sufferance
(Requisitioned as They Are)."

**"Gradual Dissolve: Three Views of Eakins's
Photographic Portrait of Whitman"**: "Straw-colored and other
psyches" is from Walt Whitman's chronicle of the Civil War,
Specimen Days:

> Aug. 4—A pretty sight! Where I sit in the shade—a
> warm day, the sun shining from cloudless skies, the
> forenoon well advanced—I look over a ten-acre field
> of luxuriant clover hay (the second crop)—the livid

ripe red blossoms and dabs of august brown thickly
spotting the prevailing green. Over all flutter myriads
of light yellow butterflies, mostly skimming over the
surface, dipping and oscillating, giving a curious
animation to the scene. The beautiful, spiritual
insects! Straw-colored and other psyches.

"Paper Ghost": Harunobu developed a form of
printmaking referred to as *ukiyo-e,* "brocade pictures." The colors
listed on line six are transliterated from Japanese: *Kiiro* is yellow,
kuro black, and *midori* green. These colors predominate in his
prints.

"Written in Hair": A sampler, which an eighteenth-
century American girl had sewn with her own hair, read, "I write
this to be remembered someday when I am gone."

"Homage to Alan Turing": At the University of
Cambridge, the young mathematician Alan Turing conceived the
fundamental principle of the modern computer. This concept did
not become a reality until after Turing's contribution to the Allied
victory in World War II, when he broke the Nazis' Enigma code.

Turing took his life in 1954. Homosexuality was illegal in
the UK at the time; it was decriminalized in 1967.

"Cocytus—River of Lamentation": Transliterated from
Modern Greek, *"Chare mou, / pare me,"* means, "Charon, take me."

Chare is the vocative case of *Charos*, the Modern Greek name for Charon—the deity who ferried the shades across the river Styx.

     "Siena" responds to Adam Zagajewski's poem "To Go to Lvov." In a letter from Parma, Francesco Petrarch writes on the aftermath of the plague:

> Where are the beloved faces? Where are the affectionate words, the relaxed and enjoyable conversations? What lightning bolt devoured them? There was a crowd of us, now we are almost alone. We should make new friends—but how, when the human race is almost wiped out, and why, when it looks to me as if the end of the world is at hand? Why pretend?

DEAN KOSTOS is the author of four poetry collections, as well as the editor of *Pomegranate Seeds: An Anthology of Greek-American Poetry* (the debut reading of which was held at the UN) and the co-editor of *Mama's Boy: Gay Men Write about Their Mothers* (a Lambda Book Award Finalist). His poems, personal essays, and translations have appeared in over 250 leading periodicals and anthologies, including *Boulevard*, *Western Humanities Review*, *Southwest Review*, *Stand Magazine* (UK), *Talisman*, and on Oprah Winfrey's Web site *Oxygen. com*. Kostos wrote the libretto *Dialogue: Angel of Peace, Angel of War*, set to music by James Bassi and performed by Voices of Ascension. Kostos's play *Box-Triptych* was performed at La Mama ETC. His literary criticism has appeared on the Harvard University Press Web site, in *American Book Review*, and elsewhere. An editor for *Journal of the Hellenic Diaspora*, he coordinated a Greek poetry event for the Rockefeller Foundation. A presenter at the Columbia Scholastic Press Association, he has also served as literary judge for Columbia University's Gold Crown and Gold Circle Awards. He has taught at Wesleyan, the Gallatin School of NYU, Teachers & Writers Collaborative, and Gotham Writers' Workshop. He is currently on the faculty of The City University of New York and Berkeley College. Trained initially as a visual artist, his works have been exhibited in galleries and at the Brooklyn Museum.

photo: Sofia Kontogeorge Kostos

My enduring gratitude to Joel Allegretti, Martine Bellen, Star Black, Alfred Corn, Walter Holland, Richard Howard, Barbara Lekatsas, Karen Neuberg, Sharon Olinka, Nicholas Samaras, Susan Wheeler, and Michael T. Young for their invaluable counsel. Special thanks to Tod Thilleman for his collegial support. DK

S PUYTEN **D** UYVIL
Meeting Eyes Bindery
Triton
Lithic Scatter

A World of Nothing But Self-Infliction Tod Thilleman

Wreckage of Reason (ed.) Nava Renek

Xian Dyad Jason Price Everett

The Yellow House Robin Behn

You, Me, and the Insects Barbara Henning

www.ingramcontent.com/pod-product-compliance
Lightning Source LLC
Chambersburg PA
CBHW020906090426
42736CB00008B/510